THE SHAWNEE

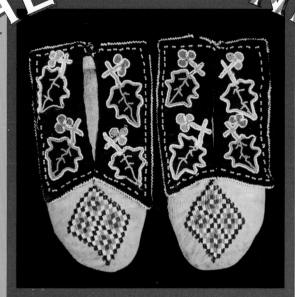

A TRUE BOOK

by

Alice K. Flanagan

Children's Press®
A Division of Scholastic Inc.

New York Toronto London Auckland Sydney
Mexico City New Delhi Hong Kong
Danbury, Connecticut

Reading Consultant
Linda Cornwell
Learning Resource Consultant
Indiana Department
of Education

A Shawnee dancer

Library of Congress Cataloging-in-Publication Data

Flanagan, Alice K.
    The Shawnee / by Alice K. Flanagan.
        p.   cm. — (A True book)
    Includes bibliographical references and index.
    Summary: Introduces the history, social structure, daily life, and culture
of the Shawnee Nation.
    ISBN 0–516–20627-3 (lib. bdg.)   0-516-26384-6 (pbk.)
    1. Shawnee Indians—History—Juvenile literature. 2. Shawnee
Indians—Social life and customs—Juvenile literature. [1. Shawnee
Indians. 2. Indians of North America—East (U.S.)] I. Title. II. Series.
E99.S35F53 1998
973'.04973—dc21   97–18272
                                                                                                        CIP
                                                                                                        AC

CHILDREN'S PRESS, AND A TRUE BOOK®, and associated logos are
trademarks and or registered trademarks of Grolier Publishing Co., Inc.
SCHOLASTIC and associated logos are trademarks and or registered
trademarks of Scholastic Inc.

4 5 6 7 8 9 0 R 07 06 05 04 03

Contents

Long ago, the Shawnee made their home in the lush, green forests of eastern North America.

The Shawnee Nation

Centuries ago, five great divisions of the Shawnee Nation lived along the Cumberland, Ohio, and Tennessee rivers in northeastern United States. They shared forests with other Eastern Woodland tribes. Over time, they formed bonds of friendship with the Delaware,

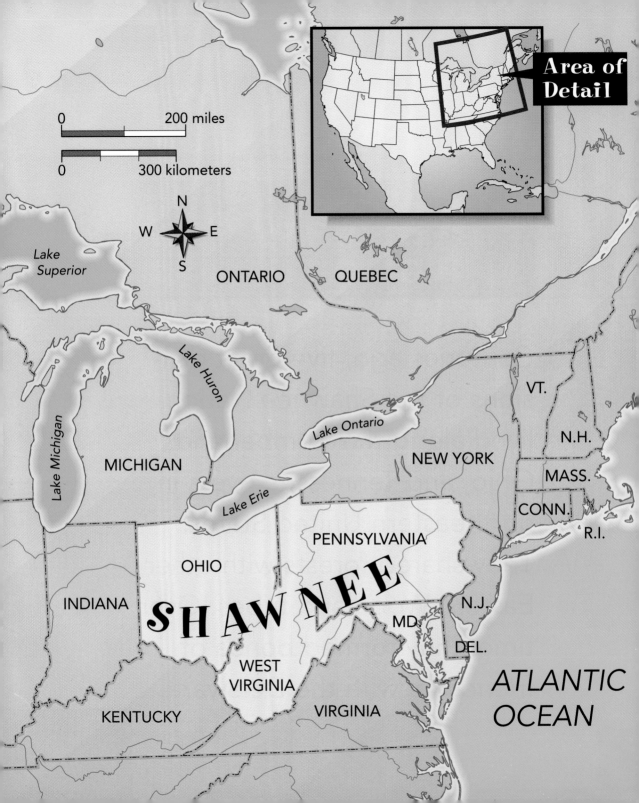

Area of
Detail

0 — 200 miles

0 — 300 kilometers

N
W E
S

Lake
Superior

ONTARIO   QUEBEC

Lake Huron

Lake Ontario

VT.

N.H.

MASS.

Lake Erie

NEW YORK

CONN.

R.I.

Lake Michigan

MICHIGAN

PENNSYLVANIA

OHIO

N.J.

SHAWNEE

MD

INDIANA

DEL.

WEST
VIRGINIA

ATLANTIC
OCEAN

KENTUCKY

VIRGINIA

Seneca, Cherokee, Creek, Caddo, Choctaw, Potawatomi, and Seminole nations. They borrowed from their cultures.

The Shawnee were nomads. They moved often and frequently split up into different groups. Because of their way of life, it is difficult to say where the first Shawnee settlements began. Remains of the oldest-known Shawnee site in North America, however, show that ancestors of the

Shawnee lived in the Ohio and Cumberland River valleys in prehistoric times.

By the time Europeans began settling North America in the 1600s, the Shawnee were living in South Carolina, Georgia, and throughout the southern states. However, after several destructive wars, Europeans and Americans took this land from them.

Today, almost 175,000 Shawnee Americans live in

Ohio, Missouri, and Oklahoma. Each is a member of one of four groups, called bands—the Loyal-Cherokee, the Absentee, the Eastern, and the United Remnant.

Each year, the Shawnee celebrate their traditions through dance and song.

Families, Bands, and Clans

The Absentee Shawnee have
their headquarters in Shawnee,
Oklahoma. The Loyal-Cherokee
Shawnee are in Tahlequah,
Oklahoma. The Eastern Shawnee
are in Seneca, Missouri, just
across the Oklahoma border.
And the United Remnant are in

The Shawnee Bands Today

① Absentee Shawnee

② Loyal-Cherokee Shawnee

③ Eastern Shawnee

④ Shawnee Nation, United Remnant

The Absentee Shawnee tribal head-quarters in Shawnee, Oklahoma

Urbana, Ohio. Each band has a chief that protects the traditions of the tribe, and a council headed by a business committee that runs the business of the tribe.

Every clan is made up
of Shawnee families.

Each band is divided into clans. A clan is a group of related families. Each clan is named in honor of an animal that guides and protects it. At birth, each person becomes a member of a clan and is known by the clan name as well as the personal name he or she was given. Some clan names are: Owl, Loon, Bear, Rabbit, Turkey, Buzzard, Horse, Snake, Turtle, Deer, Wolf or Dog, Raccoon, and Panther.

Traditional Village Life

Traditionally, Shawnee villages were built by the women. Single-family homes were made out of a frame of tree poles covered with bark. Animal skins were used as a covering when tree bark wasn't available. The summer wigwam (called a *wigi-wa*) was rectangular in shape

In the 1800s, Seth Eastman made this drawing of women from the Great Lakes region making sugar at a winter camp.

and had an arched roof. The winter home was circular with a domed roof. Later, a rectangular log cabin replaced the rough bark lodge as a winter home.

In summer, the Shawnee settled in large villages where they raised crops of corn, beans, and squash. Usually, a log structure was used as a ceremonial lodge. The Shawnee called it the Council House, or the Great House.

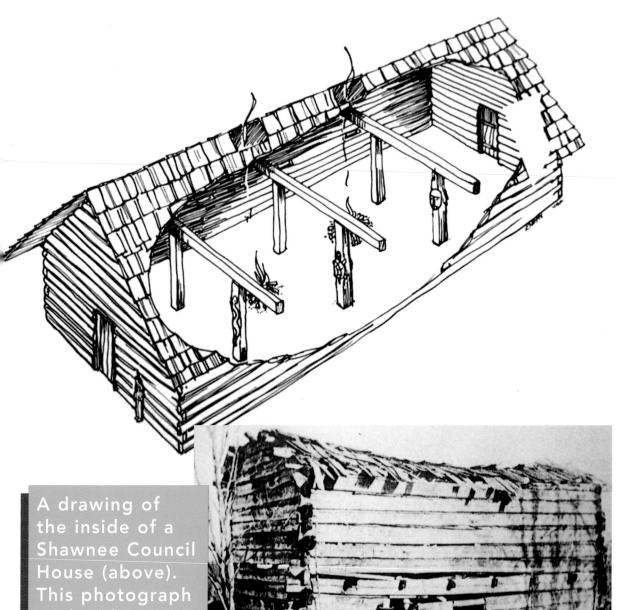

A drawing of the inside of a Shawnee Council House (above). This photograph (right) shows a Council House years after being abandoned.

Near the Council House stood the chief's lodge and the homes of the keepers of the ceremonial objects called sacred bundles. The dance grounds were nearby.

At the center of each Shawnee village were the ceremonial grounds. Built around the center were family lodges and fields of corn, beans, squash, and pumpkins. Today, the Shawnee use a similar ceremonial lodge near

In the early 1900s, a Shawnee named Ernest Spybuck painted the Shawnee ball game.

powwow grounds where they hold their yearly dances and a ceremonial ball game between men and women.

Farming and Food Gathering

As was true of most Woodland Indians, Shawnee women planted the crops and tended the fields. Corn was the most important crop. They saved the best ears of corn for seed and preserved or prepared the rest. From corn, women made hominy, which was

Shawnee women raised corn, which was an important source of food for the tribe.

like a hot cereal. Sometimes they seasoned it with meat.

From corn, women also made a variety of breads, including a delicious sour bread and blue bread. Today, the Shawnee use wheat flour to make "Indian bread" and a popular "fry bread" served at many of their gatherings.

While many of their men were away on long hunts during the winter, women made maple sugar. They collected tree sap, boiled it in large kettles, and poured it into containers to cool and harden. They collected and preserved wild plants, especially berries and nuts.

Some plants, such as onions, were dried and used for seasoning meat. Salt, which was gathered from salt springs called

Maple sugar (left) was used to sweeten foods. Berries (right) often were added to meat stews.

licks, was used, too. To add a special flavor to food, women often cooked over different kinds of woods. Hickory, maple, and wild cherry were among their favorites.

Hunting and Trapping

In late fall and winter, men hunted and trapped game. Extended trips took them into Kentucky, where there were sacred hunting grounds. Most hunters were skilled in imitating the calls of various animals. Some who were especially talented could actually call

To the Shawnee, the buffalo is a sacred animal. In the past, it provided food, shelter, warmth, and even medicine.

buffalo, deer, turkey, and panthers close enough to kill.

Immediately after the winter hunt, trapping began. The Shawnee set traps for fox, mink, rabbit, raccoon, and beaver.

In the past, Shawnee hunters spent the winter trapping beaver (above). They traded beaver skins and animal furs (left) to the Europeans.

They traded animal skins and furs for European items such as coffee, blankets, metal cook-ware, and glass beads.

Whatever hunters killed, they hung in trees and bushes away from hungry animals. They took what they could carry back to their winter camps. Within the next few days, they returned to claim what they had left behind. A good hunter never forgot the location of his catch or stole another hunter's game.

Decorative Art

The Shawnee decorated the things they made with beautiful objects, colors, and designs. They added beadwork to clothing as well as to ceremonial items. Today's Shawnee artists bead such things as collars, neck-laces, hats, and belts in addition to traditional items.

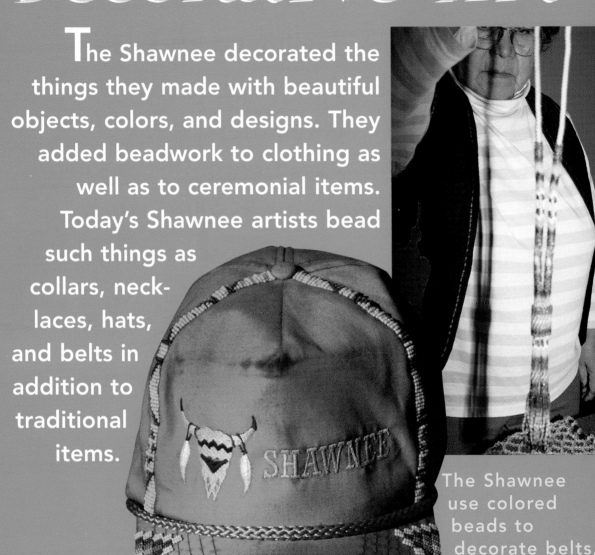

The Shawnee use colored beads to decorate belts, moccasins, and hats (left).

Men carved wooden bowls, ladles, and spoons from the knots of hardwood trees. Today, these items are rarely made. However, it was once a custom for every-one to have a wooden spoon or horn spoon to take to feasts and ceremonies.

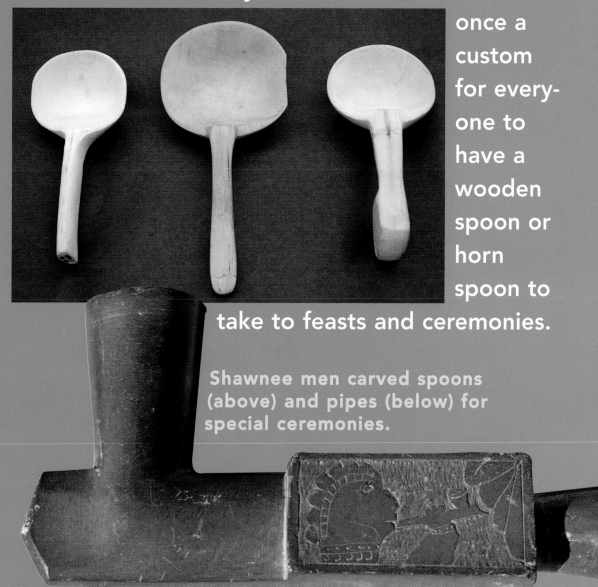

Shawnee men carved spoons (above) and pipes (below) for special ceremonies.

Celebrating the Seasons

The Shawnee celebrated each season of the year with a special dance. In March, when families began returning to the main village to prepare the fields for spring planting, they held the Spring Bread Dance. The dance honored women who

In this painting, by Ernest Spybuck, a Spring Dance is visible in the background.

provided food for the tribe. During the dance, people asked the Creator for a good growing season.

As part of the dance, the men and women played a ceremonial ball game. It was meant to bring rain to make the crops grow well. Following the game, the people planted the spring corn.

When the corn began to grow in the fields, the Shawnee held the Green Corn ceremony to thank the Creator for the first fruits of Earth. At harvest time, the Fall Bread Dance was held. It honored men who hunted for the tribe. During the dance, the people also thanked the Creator for a successful hunt.

Today, people travel great distances to participate in Shawnee dances.

Fighting to Keep a Homeland

Throughout the 1700s, Europeans and Americans fought the Shawnee and other Woodland tribes for ownership of the land on which the Indians lived and hunted. In the 1800s, a young Shawnee leader named Tecumseh tried to unite

Tecumseh (left) and Tenskwatewa (right) tried to unite various tribes into a large group called a confederacy.

the tribes and fight against those who were keeping them from the Ohio River valley. He and his brother, Tenskwatewa ("the prophet"), founded a town called Tippecanoe in Indiana Territory. Later, the town was called Prophetstown. It became a meeting place for anyone wanting to fight to protect their homeland and keep their Indian ways.

Tecumseh was a trained warrior. In the American Revolution, he fought alongside the British against American colonists. Throughout the 1790s, he fought with other Ohio tribes to stop the

American settlement from spreading. In the end, the Woodland tribes and the British were defeated.

In 1795, more than a thousand chiefs and warriors agreed to the Greenville treaty, which gave all the land south of the Ohio River (most of present-day Ohio and southern Indiana) to the United States. But Tecumseh and a few others would not sign the treaty or give up.

In 1812, Tecumseh became a general in the British army. He fought with them against Americans in the War of 1812. A year later he was killed near the Thames River in Ontario, Canada. After

Tecumseh was killed in the Battle of the Thames.

Tecumseh's death, the Shawnee gave up their fight to win back their homeland.

Kohkumthena, "Our Grandmother"

At the heart of Shawnee traditions is their belief in a Creator who watches over them. The Shawnee call the Creator Kohkumthena (go-gume-THA-na), or "Our Grandmother." According to their legend, she sits in a heavenly home weav-

ing a basket (some say a net) while she watches her Earth children from a window in the sky. At night, the dog at her side, and sometimes her grandson, unravels her weaving.

Someday, she will finish it. Then, life on earth will come to an end. "Our Grandmother" will make a new world. And into this world she will send the people she has gathered in her basket.

The Shawnee say that in the beginning, Kohkumthena gave her children a set of rules to follow. She told them to pray often and live by the sacred ways. In the past, many of these traditional beliefs were lost. Today, with Kohkumthena's guidance, the Shawnee are reclaiming them.

Today, Shawnee grandmothers watch over their families just as the Creator, Kohkumthena, does.

To Find Out More

Here are some additional resources to help you learn more about the Shawnee:

 **Books**

Landau, Elaine. **Shawnee.** Franklin Watts, 1996.

Lyback, Johanna R. **Indian Legends.** Tipi Press, 1994.

Miller, Jay. **American Indian Families.** Children's Press, 1996.

Miller, Jay. **American Indian Festivals.** Children's Press, 1996.

O'Neill, Laurie A. **Shawnee: People of the Eastern Woodlands.** Millbrook Press, 1995.

Organizations and Online Sites

First Nations Histories
http://www.tolatsga.org/ Compacts.html

A site that provides small biographies of tribes, including the Shawnee.

Native American Nations
http://www.nativeculture. com/lisamitten/nations.html

A central site that lists American Indian tribes and links to their sites.

Native American Navigator
http://www.ilt.columbia. edu/k12/naha/nanav.html

A general site with hundreds of links to topics on Native Americans.

Native Americans
http://falcon.jmu.edu/ ~ramseyil/native.htm

A site that lists groups and addresses for those interested in Native Americans.

United Tribe of Shawnee Indians
http://oz.sunflower.org/ ~hdqrs/

A small site that includes a copy of the Shawnee constitution.

Important Words

band a group of Shawnee Indians living together; there are four bands in the United States

Council House log structure in the center of the Shawnee village where important ceremonies were held

clan a group made up of related families

fry bread a popular Shawnee bread made from wheat

hominy a hot cereal made from corn

Kohkumthena Shawnee word meaning 'Our Grandmother;' the creator

Spring Bread Dance dance made in the spring to honor women and to ask the Creator for a good harvest

wigiwa a rectangular structure used by the Shawnee during the summer

Index

Meet the Author

Alice Flanagan thinks of the world as an open book filled with living stories. As an author, she thinks of herself as an observer—one who watches the stories as they unfold, then carefully writes them down.

Once a teacher, Ms. Flanagan taught Native American children in South Dakota and New Mexico. She feels blessed by the wonderful gifts they shared. Now, through her writing, she tries to pass these gifts on to others. In the True Book: Native Americans series, Ms. Flanagan is the author of the following titles. *The Eskimo, The Chippewa, The Navajo, The Nez Perce, The Pueblos, The Shawnee, The Sioux, The Tlingit, The Utes, The Wampanoags,* and *The Zunis.* Ms. Flanagan lives with her husband in Chicago, Illinois.